Let's Find Out Readers

Do the Hop!

By Janice Behrens

Do the Hop!

By Janice Behrens

No part of this publication can be reproduced in whole or in part, or stored in a retrieval system, or transmitted in any form or by any means, electronic, mechanical, photocopying, recording, or otherwise, without written permission of the publisher. For permission, write to Scholastic Inc., 557 Broadway, New York, NY 10012.

ISBN: 978-1-338-88830-0

Editor: Liza Charlesworth
Art Director: Tannaz Fassihi; Designer: Tanya Chernyak
Photos © 3: Avalon.red/Alamy Stock Photo. All other photos © Shutterstock.com.

Copyright © Scholastic Inc. All rights reserved. Published by Scholastic Inc.

1 2 3 4 5 6 7 8 9 10   68   31 30 29 28 27 26 25 24 23

Printed in Jiaxing, China. First printing, January 2023.

SCHOLASTIC INC.

Do the bunny hop!

Do the grasshoper hop!

Do the bird hop!

Do the squirrel hop!

Do the frog hop!

Do the cat hop!

Do the kid hop!

ISBN: 978-1-338-88830-0

Let's Find Out Readers

At the Pond

By Pamela Chanko

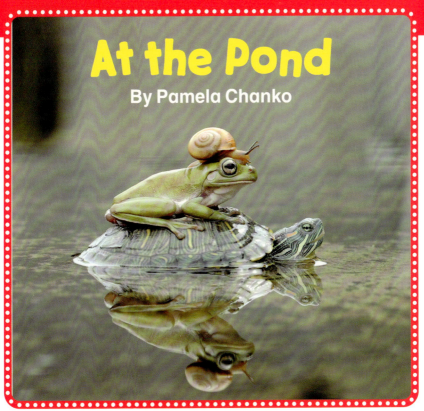

Scholastic

At the Pond

By Pamela Chanko

No part of this publication can be reproduced in whole or in part, or stored in a retrieval system, or transmitted in any form or by any means, electronic, mechanical, photocopying, recording, or otherwise, without written permission of the publisher. For permission, write to Scholastic Inc., 557 Broadway, New York, NY 10012.

ISBN: 978-1-338-88832-4

Editor: Liza Charlesworth
Art Director: Tannaz Fassihi; Designer: Tanya Chernyak
Photos ©: cover: RooM the Agency/Alamy Stock Photo; 7: Michel & Gabrielle Therin-Weise/ Alamy Stock Photo. All other photos © Shutterstock.com.

Copyright © Scholastic Inc. All rights reserved. Published by Scholastic Inc.

1 2 3 4 5 6 7 8 9 10   68   31 30 29 28 27 26 25 24 23

Printed in Jiaxing, China. First printing, January 2023.

SCHOLASTIC INC.

I see a frog!

I see a fish!

I see a turtle!

I see a duck!

I see a snail!

I see a swan!

I see a face!

Let's Find Out® Readers

ISBN: 978-1-338-88832-4

Let's Find Out Readers

Follow the Butterfly

By Pamela Chanko

Scholastic

Follow the Butterfly

By Pamela Chanko

No part of this publication can be reproduced in whole or in part, or stored in a retrieval system, or transmitted in any form or by any means, electronic, mechanical, photocopying, recording, or otherwise, without written permission of the publisher. For permission, write to Scholastic Inc., 557 Broadway, New York, NY 10012.

ISBN: 978-1-338-88834-8

Editor: Liza Charlesworth
Art Director: Tannaz Fassihi; Designer: Tanya Chernyak
Photos ©: 5: Dgwildlife/Getty Images; 7: John Dreyer/Getty Images; 8: ballycroy/Getty Images.
All other photos © Shutterstock.com.

Copyright © Scholastic Inc. All rights reserved. Published by Scholastic Inc.

1 2 3 4 5 6 7 8 9 10   68   31 30 29 28 27 26 25 24 23

Printed in Jiaxing, China. First printing, January 2023.

SCHOLASTIC INC.

It lands on a leaf.

It lands on a dog.

It lands on a cat.

It lands on a bunny.

It lands on a flower.

It lands on a tree.

It lands on me!

Let's Find Out Readers

ISBN: 978-1-338-88834-8

SCHOLASTIC

Let's Find Out Readers

What Is Frozen?

By Janice Behrens

What Is Frozen?

By Janice Behrens

No part of this publication can be reproduced in whole or in part, or stored in a retrieval system, or transmitted in any form or by any means, electronic, mechanical, photocopying, recording, or otherwise, without written permission of the publisher. For permission, write to Scholastic Inc., 557 Broadway, New York, NY 10012.

ISBN: 978-1-338-88833-1

Editor: Liza Charlesworth
Art Director: Tannaz Fassihi; Designer: Tanya Chernyak
Photos ©: cover: Tayyab Sayyad/EyeEm/Getty Images; 2: Tanaphong/Getty Images; 3: Studio CP/Getty Images; 5 icicle: borchee/Getty Images; 6-7: Ascent Xmedia/Getty Images. All other photos © Shutterstock.com.

Copyright © Scholastic Inc. All rights reserved. Published by Scholastic Inc.

1 2 3 4 5 6 7 8 9 10   68   31 30 29 28 27 26 25 24 23

Printed in Jiaxing, China. First printing, January 2023.

SCHOLASTIC INC.

The ice cube is frozen.

The ice pop is frozen.

The food is frozen.

The icicle is frozen.

The lake is frozen.

The snowman is frozen.

Let's Find Out® Readers

ISBN: 978-1-338-88833-

SCHOLASTIC

9 781338 888331

Let's Find Out Readers

Colorful Leaves

By Janice Behrens

Colorful Leaves

By Janice Behrens

No part of this publication can be reproduced in whole or in part, or stored in a retrieval system, or transmitted in any form or by any means, electronic, mechanical, photocopying, recording, or otherwise, without written permission of the publisher. For permission, write to Scholastic Inc., 557 Broadway, New York, NY 10012.

ISBN: 978-1-338-88831-7

Editor: Liza Charlesworth
Art Director: Tannaz Fassihi; Designer: Tanya Chernyak
Photos ©: 3: FatCamera/Getty Images; 5: sduben/Getty Images.
All other photos © Shutterstock.com.

Copyright © Scholastic Inc. All rights reserved. Published by Scholastic Inc.

1 2 3 4 5 6 7 8 9 10   68   31 30 29 28 27 26 25 24 23

Printed in Jiaxing, China. First printing, January 2023.

SCHOLASTIC INC.

Red leaves fall down.

Brown leaves fall down.

Orange leaves fall down.

Purple leaves fall down.

Yellow leaves fall down.

Colorful leaves fall down.

Let's Find Out® Readers

ISBN: 978-1-338-88831-

SCHOLASTIC

9 781338 888317

Let's Find Out Readers

Baby Animal School

By Pamela Chanko

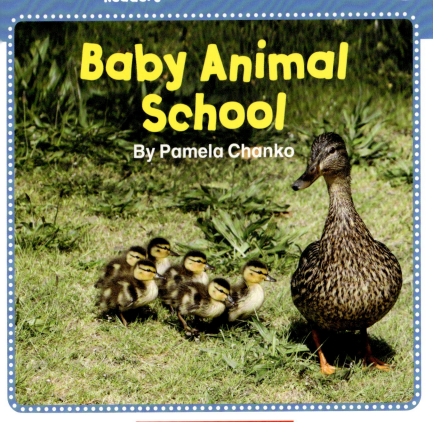

SCHOLASTIC

Baby Animal School

By Pamela Chanko

No part of this publication can be reproduced in whole or in part, or stored in a retrieval system, or transmitted in any form or by any means, electronic, mechanical, photocopying, recording, or otherwise, without written permission of the publisher. For permission, write to Scholastic Inc., 557 Broadway, New York, NY 10012.

ISBN: 978-1-338-88835-5

Editor: Liza Charlesworth
Art Director: Tannaz Fassihi; Designer: Tanya Chernyak
Photos ©: 2: Pascale Gueret/Alamy Stock Photo; 5: imageBROKER/Alamy Stock Photo; 7: JohnCarnemolla/Getty Images. All other photos © Shutterstock.com.

Copyright © Scholastic Inc. All rights reserved. Published by Scholastic Inc.

1 2 3 4 5 6 7 8 9 10   68   31 30 29 28 27 26 25 24 23

Printed in Jiaxing, China. First printing, January 2023.

SCHOLASTIC INC.

Baby animals learn to walk.
Walk, walk!

Baby animals learn to swim.
Swim, swim!

Baby animals learn to run.
Run, run!

Baby animals learn to play.
Play, play!

Baby animals learn to climb.
Climb, climb!

Baby animals learn to hop.
Hop, hop!

Baby animals learn to nap.
Nap, nap!

Let's Find Out
Readers

ISBN: 978-1-338-88835-

SCHOLASTIC

Let's Find Out Readers

Tall, Tall Sunflowers

By Janice Behrens

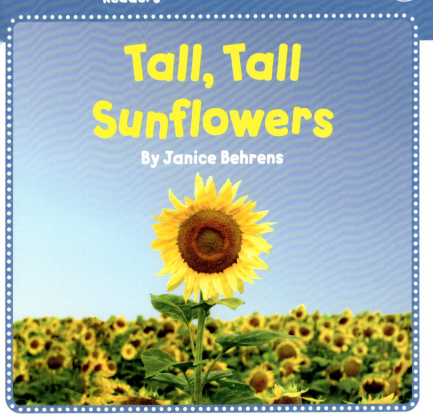

Scholastic

Tall, Tall Sunflowers

By Janice Behrens

No part of this publication can be reproduced in whole or in part, or stored in a retrieval system, or transmitted in any form or by any means, electronic, mechanical, photocopying, recording, or otherwise, without written permission of the publisher. For permission, write to Scholastic Inc., 557 Broadway, New York, NY 10012.

ISBN: 978-1-338-88838-6

Editor: Liza Charlesworth
Art Director: Tannaz Fassihi; Designer: Tanya Chernyak
Photos ©: cover: Samlyn_Studio/Getty Images; 2: HollyAA/Getty Images; 3: baza178/Getty Images; 6: Rimmochkaivanova00/Dreamstime; 7: borissos/123RF; 8: taxihiro/Getty Images. All other photos © Shutterstock.com.

Copyright © Scholastic Inc. All rights reserved. Published by Scholastic Inc.

1 2 3 4 5 6 7 8 9 10   68   31 30 29 28 27 26 25 24 23

Printed in Jiaxing, China. First printing, January 2023.

SCHOLASTIC INC.

Can they be taller than a dog?
Yes, they can.

Can they be taller than a fence?
Yes, they can.

Can they be taller than a tractor?
Yes, they can.

Can they be taller than a cow?
Yes, they can.

Can they be taller than a sign?
Yes, they can.

Can they be taller than a kid?
Yes, they can.

Tall, tall sunflowers!

Let's Find Out® Readers

ISBN: 978-1-338-88838-

SCHOLASTIC

9 781338 888386

Let's Find Out Readers

Thank You, Trees!
By Pamela Chanko

Scholastic

Thank You, Trees!

By Pamela Chanko

No part of this publication can be reproduced in whole or in part, or stored in a retrieval system, or transmitted in any form or by any means, electronic, mechanical, photocopying, recording, or otherwise, without written permission of the publisher. For permission, write to Scholastic Inc., 557 Broadway, New York, NY 10012.

ISBN: 978-1-338-88836-2

Editor: Liza Charlesworth
Art Director: Tannaz Fassihi; Designer: Tanya Chernyak
Photos © Shutterstock.com.

Copyright © Scholastic Inc. All rights reserved. Published by Scholastic Inc.

1 2 3 4 5 6 7 8 9 10   68   31 30 29 28 27 26 25 24 23

Printed in Jiaxing, China. First printing, January 2023.

SCHOLASTIC INC.

Apples come from trees.
Thank you, trees!

Oranges come from trees.
Thank you, trees!

Peaches come from trees.
Thank you, trees!

Lemons come from trees.
Thank you, trees!

Cherries come from trees.
Thank you, trees!

Pears come from trees.
Thank you, trees!

Yum, yum, yum!
Thank you, trees!

Let's Find Out Readers

ISBN: 978-1-338-88836-

Let's Find Out Readers

Who Eats Plants?

By Pamela Chanko

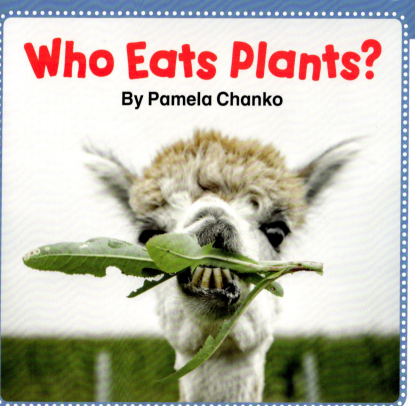

SCHOLASTIC

Who Eats Plants?

By Pamela Chanko

No part of this publication can be reproduced in whole or in part, or stored in a retrieval system, or transmitted in any form or by any means, electronic, mechanical, photocopying, recording, or otherwise, without written permission of the publisher. For permission, write to Scholastic Inc., 557 Broadway, New York, NY 10012.

ISBN: 978-1-338-88837-9

Editor: Liza Charlesworth
Art Director: Tannaz Fassihi; Designer: Tanya Chernyak
Photos ©: cover: Ken Gillespie Photography/Alamy Stock Photo; 2: mashabuba/Getty Images; 3: Ken Gillespie Photography/Alamy Stock Photo; 4: Simon Gardner/Media Bakery; 6: mihtiander/Getty Images. All other photos © Shutterstock.com.

Copyright © Scholastic Inc. All rights reserved. Published by Scholastic Inc.

1 2 3 4 5 6 7 8 9 10   68   31 30 29 28 27 26 25 24 23

Printed in Jiaxing, China. First printing, January 2023.

SCHOLASTIC INC.

A bunny eats plants.
Crunch, crunch!

A deer eats plants.
Crunch, crunch!

A woodchuck eats plants.
Crunch, crunch!

A giraffe eats plants.
Crunch, crunch!

A goat eats plants.
Crunch, crunch!

A panda eats plants.
Crunch, crunch!

We eat plants.
Mmm, lunch!

Let's Find Out® Readers

ISBN: 978-1-338-88837-9

SCHOLASTIC

Let's Find Out Readers

Winter Sleepers

By Janice Behrens

Zzzz.

SCHOLASTIC

Winter Sleepers

By Janice Behrens

No part of this publication can be reproduced in whole or in part, or stored in a retrieval system, or transmitted in any form or by any means, electronic, mechanical, photocopying, recording, or otherwise, without written permission of the publisher. For permission, write to Scholastic Inc., 557 Broadway, New York, NY 10012.

ISBN: 978-1-338-88839-3

Editor: Liza Charlesworth
Art Director: Tannaz Fassihi; Designer: Tanya Chernyak
Photos ©: cover: Paul Souders/Getty Images; 2: Breck Kent/Animals Animals; 4: Remus86/Getty Images; 8: All Canada Photos/Alamy Stock Photo. All other photos © Shutterstock.com.

Copyright © Scholastic Inc. All rights reserved. Published by Scholastic Inc.

1 2 3 4 5 6 7 8 9 10   68   31 30 29 28 27 26 25 24 23

Printed in Jiaxing, China. First printing, January 2023.

SCHOLASTIC INC.

It is time to sleep.
"Zzzz," said the mouse.

It is time to sleep.
"Zzzz," said the ladybug.

It is time to sleep.
"Zzzz," said the bat.

It is time to sleep.
"Zzzz," said the frog.

It is time to sleep.
"Zzzz," said the snail.

It is time to sleep,
"Zzzz," said the turtle.

It is time to sleep.
"Zzzz," said the bear.
"Grrr!" said the cub.

Let's Find Out
Readers

ISBN: 978-1-338-88839-

SCHOLASTIC

Let's Find Out Readers

Listen to the Weather

By Pamela Chanko

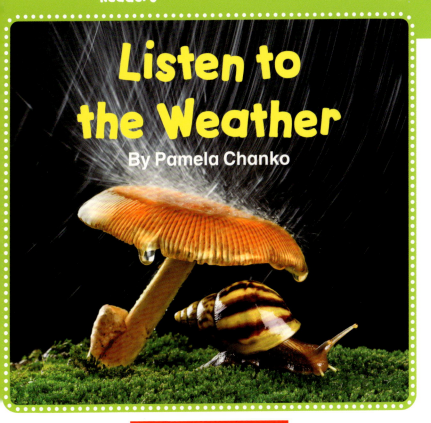

SCHOLASTIC

Listen to the Weather

By Pamela Chanko

No part of this publication can be reproduced in whole or in part, or stored in a retrieval system, or transmitted in any form or by any means, electronic, mechanical, photocopying, recording, or otherwise, without written permission of the publisher. For permission, write to Scholastic Inc., 557 Broadway, New York, NY 10012.

ISBN: 978-1-338-88842-3

Editor: Liza Charlesworth
Art Director: Tannaz Fassihi; Designer: Tanya Chernyak
Photos ©: cover: Arthit Somsakul/Getty Images; 4: kozorog/Getty Images; 6: Susan Feldberg/Alamy Stock Photo; 7: Merrimon/Getty Images; 8 background: yanikap/Getty Images.
All other photos © Shutterstock.com.

Copyright © Scholastic Inc. All rights reserved. Published by Scholastic Inc.

1 2 3 4 5 6 7 8 9 10   68   31 30 29 28 27 26 25 24 23

Printed in Jinxing, China. First printing, January 2023.

SCHOLASTIC INC.

Can you hear the rain?
Drip, drip!

Can you hear the wind?
Whoosh, whoosh!

Can you hear the thunder?

Boom, boom!

Can you hear the snow?
Flutter, flutter!

Can you hear the ice?
Slip, slip!

Can you hear the clouds?
Shh, Shh!

ISBN: 978-1-338-88842-1

SCHOLASTIC

Squirrel's Nut Hunt

By Janice Behrens

Squirrel's Nut Hunt

By Janice Behrens

No part of this publication can be reproduced in whole or in part, or stored in a retrieval system, or transmitted in any form or by any means, electronic, mechanical, photocopying, recording, or otherwise, without written permission of the publisher. For permission, write to Scholastic Inc., 557 Broadway, New York, NY 10012.

ISBN: 978-1-338-88840-9

Editor: Liza Charlesworth
Art Director: Tannaz Fassihi; Designer: Tanya Chernyak
Photos ©: cover: suefeldberg/Getty Images; 2: schnuddel/Getty Images; 3: bigemrg/Getty Images; 4: Carol Hamilton/Getty Images; 5: JoeDunckley/Getty Images; 6: Menno Schaefer/Shutterstock; 7: Michael_Conrad/Getty Images; 8: Steven Cooper/Alamy Stock Photo.

Copyright © Scholastic Inc. All rights reserved. Published by Scholastic Inc.

1 2 3 4 5 6 7 8 9 10   68   31 30 29 28 27 26 25 24 23

Printed in Jiaxing, China. First printing, January 2023.

SCHOLASTIC INC.

This squirrel looked in the flowers. It did not find nuts.

This squirrel looked on the fence.
It did not find nuts.

This squirrel looked in the pumpkin.
It did not find nuts.

This squirrel looked on the bench.
It did not find nuts.

This squirrel looked in the can.
It did not find nuts.

This squirrel looked on the stump.
It DID find nuts!

Crunch, crunch!
Crunch, crunch!

ISBN: 978-1-338-88840-9

Scholastic

9 781338 888409

Who Is Hatching?

By Janice Behrens

Who Is Hatching?

By Janice Behrens

No part of this publication can be reproduced in whole or in part, or stored in a retrieval system, or transmitted in any form or by any means, electronic, mechanical, photocopying, recording, or otherwise, without written permission of the publisher. For permission, write to Scholastic Inc., 557 Broadway, New York, NY 10012.

ISBN: 978-1-338-88841-6

Editor: Liza Charlesworth
Art Director: Tannaz Fassihi; Designer: Tanya Chernyak
Photos ©: 2: Dorling Kindersley ltd/Alamy Stock Photo; 2 inset: Antagain/Getty Images; 4: FLPA/Alamy Stock Photo; 4 inset: Mark Kostich/Getty Images; 5 main: Westend61 on Offset/Shutterstock; 6: Ingo Arndt/NPL/Minden Pictures; 6 inset: KenCanning/Getty Images; 7 main: RooM the Agency/Alamy Stock Photo; 8: Stepanyda/Getty Images; 8 inset: aluxum/Getty Images.
All other photos © Shutterstock.com.

Copyright © Scholastic Inc. All rights reserved. Published by Scholastic Inc.

1 2 3 4 5 6 7 8 9 10   68   31 30 29 28 27 26 25 24 23

Printed in Jiaxing, China. First printing, January 2023.

SCHOLASTIC INC.

Crack, crack!
A little baby is hatching.
It will grow up to be a big duck.

Crack, crack!
A little baby is hatching.
It will grow up to be a big crocodile.

Crack, crack!
A little baby is hatching.
It will grow up to be a big snake!

Crack, crack!
A little baby is hatching.
It will grow up to be a big tortoise!

Crack, crack!
A little baby is hatching.
It will grow up to be a big ostrich!

Crack, crack!
A little baby is hatching.
It will grow up to be a big lizard!

Crack, crack!
A little baby is hatching.
It will grow up to be a big hen.
Then it can lay an egg!

Let's Find Out Readers

ISBN: 978-1-338-88841-

Scholastic

9 781338 888416

In the Tree

By Pamela Chanko

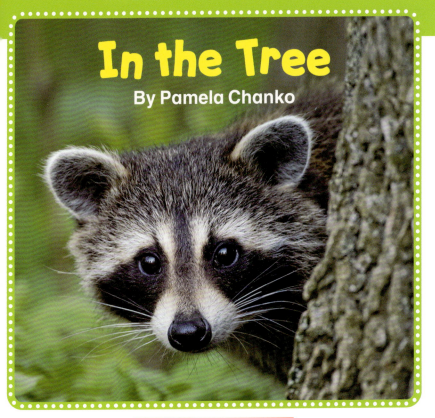

In the Tree

By Pamela Chanko

No part of this publication can be reproduced in whole or in part, or stored in a retrieval system, or transmitted in any form or by any means, electronic, mechanical, photocopying, recording, or otherwise, without written permission of the publisher. For permission, write to Scholastic Inc., 557 Broadway, New York, NY 10012.

ISBN: 978-1-338-88843-0

Editor: Liza Charlesworth
Art Director: Tannaz Fassihi; Designer: Tanya Chernyak
Photos © Shutterstock.com.

Copyright © Scholastic Inc. All rights reserved. Published by Scholastic Inc.

1 2 3 4 5 6 7 8 9 10   68   31 30 29 28 27 26 25 24 23

Printed in Jiaxing, China. First printing, January 2023.

SCHOLASTIC INC.

Who is in the tree?
A bird is in the tree.

Who is in the tree?
A raccoon is in the tree.

Who is in the tree?
A squirrel is in the tree.

Who is in the tree?
A fox is in the tree.

Who is in the tree?
A bat is in the tree.

Who is in the tree?
A cat is in the tree.

Come down, cat!
Come down to me!

ISBN: 978-1-338-88843-

Let's Find Out Readers

A Little Ladybug

By Janice Behrens

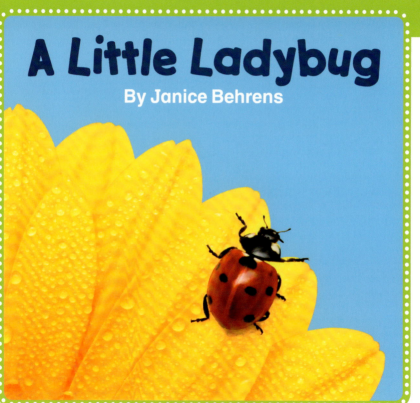

SCHOLASTIC

A Little Ladybug

By Janice Behrens

No part of this publication can be reproduced in whole or in part, or stored in a retrieval system, or transmitted in any form or by any means, electronic, mechanical, photocopying, recording, or otherwise, without written permission of the publisher. For permission, write to Scholastic Inc., 557 Broadway, New York, NY 10012.

ISBN: 978-1-338-88844-7

Editor: Liza Charlesworth
Art Director: Tannaz Fassihi; Designer: Tanya Chernyak
Photos ©: cover: Maceofoto/Shutterstock; 2: Avalon_Studio/Getty Images; 3: AlpamayoPhoto/Getty Images; 4-5: Yurich84/Getty Images; 6: iwka/Getty Images; 7: kislev/Getty Images; 8: Tutye/Getty Images.

Copyright © Scholastic Inc. All rights reserved. Published by Scholastic Inc.

1 2 3 4 5 6 7 8 9 10   68   31 30 29 28 27 26 25 24 23

Printed in Jiaxing, China. First printing, January 2023.

SCHOLASTIC INC.

I spy a little ladybug.
Where will it go?

It goes on a flower.
Crawl, crawl!

It goes on a branch.

Crawl, crawl!

It goes on an apple.
Crawl, crawl!

It goes on a finger.
Crawl, crawl!

It goes away forever.
Bye-bye!

Let's Find Out Readers

ISBN: 978-1-338-88844-

9 781338 888447

D

How Do Animals Say Hello?

By Pamela Chanko

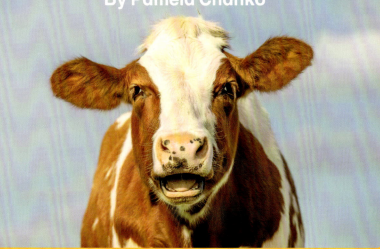

Scholastic

How Do Animals Say Hello?

By Pamela Chanko

No part of this publication can be reproduced in whole or in part, or stored in a retrieval system, or transmitted in any form or by any means, electronic, mechanical, photocopying, recording, or otherwise, without written permission of the publisher. For permission, write to Scholastic Inc., 557 Broadway, New York, NY 10012.

ISBN: 978-1-338-88845-4

Editor: Liza Charlesworth
Art Director: Tannaz Fassihi; Designer: Tanya Chernyak
Photos ©: 2: Mint Images Limited/Alamy Stock Photo; 7: F1online digitale Bildagentur GmbH/Alamy Stock Photo; 8: Freder/Getty Images. All other photos © Shutterstock.com.

Copyright © Scholastic Inc. All rights reserved. Published by Scholastic Inc.

1 2 3 4 5 6 7 8 9 10   68   31 30 29 28 27 26 25 24 23

Printed in Jiaxing, China. First printing, January 2023.

SCHOLASTIC INC.

How does a pig
say hello to you?
It says, "Oink!"
Hello, pink pig!

How does a cow
say hello to you?
It says, "Moo!"
Hello, spotted cow!

How does a lamb
say hello to you?
It says, "Baa!"
Hello, fuzzy lamb!

How does a horse
say hello to you?
It says, "Neigh!"
Hello, big horse!

How does a duck
say hello to you?
It says, "Quack!"
Hello, wet duck!

How does a chick
say hello to you?
It says, "Peep!"
Hello, cute chick!

How does a rooster
say hello to you?
It says, "COCK-A-DOODLE-DO!"
Hello, loud rooster!

Let's Find Out® Readers

ISBN: 978-1-338-88845-

SCHOLASTIC

9 781338 888454

If You Were a Frog

By Janice Behrens

SCHOLASTIC

If You Were a Frog

By Janice Behrens

No part of this publication can be reproduced in whole or in part, or stored in a retrieval system, or transmitted in any form or by any means, electronic, mechanical, photocopying, recording, or otherwise, without written permission of the publisher. For permission, write to Scholastic Inc., 557 Broadway, New York, NY 10012.

ISBN: 978-1-338-88848-5

Editor: Liza Charlesworth
Art Director: Tannaz Fassihi; Designer: Tanya Chernyak
Photos ©: cover: BrianLasenby/Getty Images; 4: Joe McDonald/Getty Images; 5: Buddy Mays/Alamy Stock Photo; 6: Herman Bresser/Getty Images; 7: taviphoto/Getty Images; 8: real444/Getty Images. All other photos © Shutterstock.com.

Copyright © Scholastic Inc. All rights reserved. Published by Scholastic Inc.

1 2 3 4 5 6 7 8 9 10   68   31 30 29 28 27 26 25 24 23

Printed in Jiaxing, China. First printing, January 2023.

SCHOLASTIC INC.

If you were a frog,
you could hop, hop, hop.
Would you like to do that?

If you were a frog,
you could swim, swim, swim.
Would you like to do that?

If you were a frog,
you could hide in a pond.
Would you like to do that?

If you were a frog,
you could eat a big bug.
Would you like to do that?

If you were a frog,
you could sit on a rock.
Would you like to do that?

If you were a frog,
you could hang on a twig.
Would you like to do that?

If you were a frog,
you could say, "Ribbit!"
Would you like to do that?

ISBN: 978-1-338-88848-5

SCHOLASTIC

D

I See Shapes

By Janice Behrens

Scholastic

I See Shapes

By Janice Behrens

No part of this publication can be reproduced in whole or in part, or stored in a retrieval system, or transmitted in any form or by any means, electronic, mechanical, photocopying, recording, or otherwise, without written permission of the publisher. For permission, write to Scholastic Inc., 557 Broadway, New York, NY 10012.

ISBN: 978-1-338-88846-1

Editor: Liza Charlesworth
Art Director: Tannaz Fassihi; Designer: Tanya Chernyak
Photos ©: cover: Darrell Gulin/Getty Images; 2: DanielPrudek/Getty Images; 3: Insung Jeon/Getty Images; 8: fortise/Getty Images. All other photos © Shutterstock.com.

Copyright © Scholastic Inc. All rights reserved. Published by Scholastic Inc.

1 2 3 4 5 6 7 8 9 10   68   31 30 29 28 27 26 25 24 23

Printed in Jiaxing, China. First printing, January 2023.

SCHOLASTIC INC.

The shape of this mountain
is easy to see.
It looks like a triangle to me.

The shape of this field
is easy to see.
It looks like a square to me.

The shape of this leaf
is easy to see.
It looks like a circle to me.

The shape of this stone
is easy to see.
It looks like a rectangle to me.

star

The shape of this sea star
is easy to see.
It looks like a star to me.

The shape of this egg
is easy to see.
It looks like an oval to me.

The shape of this flower
is easy to see.
It looks like a heart to me.

ISBN: 978-1-338-88846-1

Let's Find Out Readers

D

Is It Spring?

By Pamela Chanko

Scholastic

Is It Spring?
By Pamela Chanko

No part of this publication can be reproduced in whole or in part, or stored in a retrieval system, or transmitted in any form or by any means, electronic, mechanical, photocopying, recording, or otherwise, without written permission of the publisher. For permission, write to Scholastic Inc., 557 Broadway, New York, NY 10012.

ISBN: 978-1-338-88849-2

Editor: Liza Charlesworth
Art Director: Tannaz Fassihi; Designer: Tanya Chernyak
Photos ©: 2: connect11/Getty Images; 7: Arterra Picture Library/Alamy Stock Photo;
8: pat138241/Getty Images. All other photos © Shutterstock.com.

Copyright © Scholastic Inc. All rights reserved. Published by Scholastic Inc.

1 2 3 4 5 6 7 8 9 10   68   31 30 29 28 27 26 25 24 23

Printed in Jiaxing, China. First printing, January 2023.

SCHOLASTIC INC.

Is it spring?
Look for a clue.
I see a green frog.
Do you see it, too?

Is it spring?
Look for a clue.
I see a fluffy bunny.
Do you see it, too?

Is it spring?
Look for a clue.
I see a pretty flower.
Do you see it, too?

Is it spring?
Look for a clue.
I see a blue bird.
Do you see it, too?

Is it spring?
Look for a clue.
I see a buzzing bee.
Do you see it, too?

Is it spring?
Look for a clue.
I see a wiggly worm.
Do you see it, too?

Is it spring?
Look for a clue.
I see a happy kid.
Do you see her, too?

ISBN: 978-1-338-88849-2

Let's Find Out Readers

D

What Can Wind Do?

By Pamela Chanko

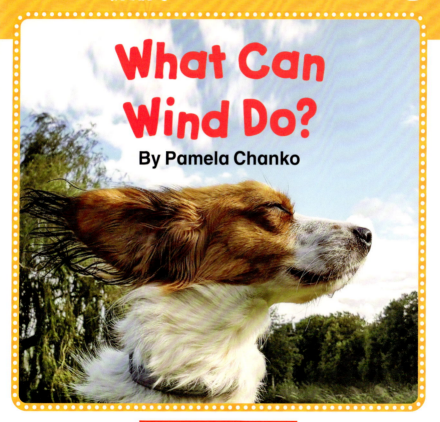

SCHOLASTIC

What Can Wind Do?

By Pamela Chanko

No part of this publication can be reproduced in whole or in part, or stored in a retrieval system, or transmitted in any form or by any means, electronic, mechanical, photocopying, recording, or otherwise, without written permission of the publisher. For permission, write to Scholastic Inc., 557 Broadway, New York, NY 10012.

ISBN: 978-1-338-88847-8

Editor: Liza Charlesworth
Art Director: Tannaz Fassihi; Designer: Tanya Chernyak
Photos ©: 2: Fuse/Getty Images; 3: RomoloTavani/Getty Images; 5: katerinchik73/Getty Images; 6-7: Erickson Stock/Alamy Stock Photo; 8: RooM the Agency/Alamy Stock Photo.
All other photos © Shutterstock.com.

Copyright © Scholastic Inc. All rights reserved. Published by Scholastic Inc.

1 2 3 4 5 6 7 8 9 10   68   31 30 29 28 27 26 25 24 23

Printed in Jiaxing, China. First printing, January 2023.

SCHOLASTIC INC.

Wind can make your hair blow.
"Whoosh!" goes the wind.

Wind can make these seeds go.
"Whoosh!" goes the wind.

Wind can make a kite fly.
"Whoosh!" goes the wind.

Wind can make a boat sail by.
"Whoosh!" goes the wind.

Wind can make the trees sway.
"Whoosh!" goes the wind.

What else happens on a windy day?

Wind can take your hat away!
"Whoosh!" goes the wind.

ISBN: 978-1-338-88847-8